Operating

the

BBC Microcomputer

———

A Concise Guide

Graham Leah

M

First published 1985.
Published by
MACMILLAN EDUCATION LTD
Houndmills, Basingstoke, Hampshire RG21 2XS
and London
Companies and representatives throughout the
world.

Printed in Great Britain by
The Camelot Press
Southampton

British Library Cataloguing in Publication Data

Leah, Graham
   Operating the BBC Microcomputer: A Concise Guide
   1. BBC Microcomputer
   I. Title
   001.64-04   QA76.8.B35

   ISBN 0-333-40687-7

CONTENTS

The official User Guide

Where possible, cross-referencing between this guide and the official User Guide have been given; these references are detailed on pages 55 and 56, and are indicated in the text by

ref * n

where ´n´ is the reference number.

However, as the User Guide has appeared in many editions, it is not always possible to indicate a precise page or section number.

I N T R O D U C T I O N

The purpose of this guide is to provide ready access to information on operating the BBC microcomputer.

All the information presented here is available from the various technical handbooks. However, locating the required information can often be a long and frustrating task - hence the advantages of this guide which may be kept alongside your micro as an easy reference book.

Usage of the procedures described becomes obvious after a few attempts, and the complete novice will soon find that many previously ´experts only´ operations become suprisingly easy to perform.

The author dedicates this guide to a machine that operates using ´0´ and ´1´ and yet is capable of making a complex human being feel a complete computer idiot!

I also give thanks to ARTHUR and JIM for their convincing portrayal of the above role!

S E T T I N G   U P

(ref *1)

It is assumed that you are aware of all the switch positions and that all your equipment is correctly wired.

It is important to switch the computer ON and OFF last of all.

Therefore:

        POWER on   disc drive
        POWER on   monitor
        POWER on   any other peripherals
        POWER on   micro

Follow the same sequence when switching off. Note that there is frequently NO power switch on the disc drive or tape player.

```
*********************
* N.B. REMOVE DISCS *
*    FROM THE DRIVE  *
* BEFORE SWITCHING   *
*       ON OR OFF.   *
*********************
```

After switching on, one of the following messages will appear:

```
BBC Computer    32K
Acorn DFS
BASIC
>
```

if you have a Disc Filing System, or

```
BBC Computer    32K
Acorn TFS
BASIC
>
```

if you have the (older) Tape Filing System.

This indicates that the machine is ready for you to begin.

D A T A   S T O R A G E   S Y S T E M S

The advantages and disadvantages of tape
storage compared to disc storage are many;
however, a summary would be:

```
          Tape slow    -  Disc quick
          Tape robust  -  Disc fragile
          Tape uncertain - Disc reliable
```

However this hides the fact that the systems
and media have different handling problems.

The tape-based system is very slow and
loading and saving can be a somewhat
hit-and-miss affair. However, the actual
storage medium (the tape) is fairly
hard-wearing and resistant to grubby paws -
although one should never touch the surface
of the tape. Tapes and players are
reasonably priced and are readily available.

By comparison the disc drives are very quick
in operation, and very costly. They are a
closed book to all but the most
technically-minded and all usage is
controlled by the computer. The discs
themselves are extremely fragile and can
easily be damaged. They are particularly
fond of refusing to give up stored programs
following a brief bend or twist from a
sticky enquiring hand.

T A P E   S T O R A G E

HANDLING

1. Although the tapes are more durable you should ensure that they are kept in a clean environment.

2. Since recording on to tape can be rather unpredictable, it is advisable to record all data and programs twice.

3. Only use cassettes designed for computer usage. Conventional ´music´ cassettes often have small gaps in the medium coverage on the tape. This will pass unnoticed in playing music but will prevent the computer from loading data properly.

The apparent cost advantage of longer tapes will ultimately prove a source of frustration when each tape contains dozens of different programs - none of which can immediately be found! Furthermore, the loss of one such tape containing many programs will clearly be more traumatic than the occasional mislaying of a tape with only one or two programs on it.

USING A TAPE LOAD/SAVE

You should know if your machine has a disc interface fitted. If you are not sure check the screen display on switching the machine on: see page 3.

If the machine has no disc interface you will not require to keep changing the filing system described below. However, if the machine powers up in DFS (disc filing system) mode and you are attempting to load from tape it is necessary to change to the TFS (tape filing system).

NOTE

ALL COMMAND WORDS
MUST BE IN UPPER CASE

This is done by typing

*TAPE (RETURN)

The * character is on the colon key with shift held down.

NOTE
IT WILL BE NECESSARY TO USE THIS COMMAND FOLLOWING ANY **BREAKS,** AS THE MACHINE RESETS TO DFS.

The machine will now LOAD or SAVE from the tape player.

LOADING FROM TAPE (ref. *2)

Having selected Tape Filing System,

1.   Load the tape player with   cassette   and
press PLAY.

The tape player will not run as the computer
controls   the   motor   of the tape player. If
fast forward or rewind is required then   the
cassette   motor   may   be   activated   by   the
commands

> *MOTOR 1   (RETURN)
> (cassette motor on)
>
> *MOTOR 0   (RETURN)
> (cassette motor off)

2.   Type in the command
>   CHAIN "program name" (RETURN).

The quote marks (shift 2) are vital.

3.   Message appears: **Searching**

4.   This should be followed by the   message:

> **Loading**   program name

5.   A   series   of   numbers   and   letters will
appear counting the bytes   of   the   program.
The   machine   stores data in blocks of audio
signals which it must load in order, without
any gaps.

PROBLEMS

If the volume on the tape is not set correctly, then it is possible that the computer will not pick up the program at all; the computer will continue to search until the end of the tape.

Rewind the tape and adjust the volume. (On some tape players the sound of the computer program will come through the loudspeaker; if the volume is high and the noise level is unacceptable, then plug in the dummy earphone plug which is usually supplied.)

Even if the loading message does appear the computer may fail to pick up the whole program. In this case one of two messages will appear:
                 ´ Block ´ or ´ Data ? ´

As before rewind tape and adjust the volume. However, it is possible that a corruption of the tape will prevent loading at any volume level and you will be glad that you have had the foresight to record a backup copy of your program (see BACKUP copying).

Persistent failure to pick up programs from tape, particularly when the programs have been recorded on another machine, is often caused by tape head alignment. It may be necessary to adjust the position of the tape head. If you are unsure of the method for adjustment consult either a computer shop or an audio equipment shop.

SAVING TO TAPE

(ref. *3)

CHECK THAT THE MACHINE IS IN TFS;
IF IN DOUBT TYPE ***TAPE** (Return)

1. Find a blank tape and wind it on, by hand, past the leader (the red tape that joins the brown magnetic medium to the spools). This is easily done using a pencil.

2. Press Record and Play together and ensure that both are engaged.

3. Type
        SAVE "program name" (RETURN)

4. Message appears:
            Record and return

5. Check that the tape player is recording, and press RETURN.

6. The computer will start the cassette motor and start to save the program.

7. Saving is complete when the screen displays the cursor >.

8. Repeat the SAVE procedure on the reverse side of the tape as a backup copy - and write the name of the program on the cassette.

PROBLEMS

A failed save may be caused by the cassette player, poor tapes or faulty connection leads.

Clean the recording heads of the player at intervals - use a special ´cloth tape´ cleaning cassette, readily available at audio stores - and ensure that you use quality tapes.

In order to safeguard any recordings you have made, press out the little plastic tongues found at the back of the cassette case. Now, no recording can be made accidentally on top of your recording.

Should you definitely wish to record over the top of such a ´protected´ recording, then simply replace the plastic tongue by placing a piece of adhesive tape over the hole.

D I S C   S T O R A G E

HANDLING

IT IS VITAL THAT ALL USERS ARE AWARE OF
CORRECT DISC HANDLING METHODS!

1. Discs are delicate !
   Hold the disc by the label ONLY.
   NEVER touch the inner disc.

2. Do not write on the disc label other than
with felt tip. (GENTLY!)

3. Do not store discs near the monitor or
any other source of magnetic fields.

4. Always return the disc to its storage
envelope as soon as it is removed from the
drive. NEVER place it on the desk.

5. Any important data or program should be
saved on to a disc which can be kept as a
Library copy in the event of the original
copy being lost or corrupted.

6. If the disc gets dust or grease on its
surface then it is likely to result in an
error message:
          Disc fault xx at sector yy.

Disc errors **may** not be critical, but they
can mean the total loss of all programs
stored on that disc.

GENERAL

It is well worthwhile purchasing the plastic
library cases which hold ten discs; they
make it easier to organise your discs, and
obviously provide greater safety -
especially if you have to move discs from
building to building.

Discs can be physically protected against
accidental over-recording in a similar way
to cassettes. On the left of the disc (as
you slide it into a horizontal disc drive)
there is a single small notch. To allow
recording this notch must be open; to
prevent recording, cover the notch with one
of the little self-adhesive tabs provided
with the discs. Always bear in mind that
any disc with this tab covering the notch
will **not** allow any FORMAT, SAVE or file
WRITE operation.

There are a variety of forms of disc drive:
single- or double-sided, 40- or 80-track.
Although the most common set-up encountered
is one single-sided, 40-track disc drive,
you may like to check - and then put the
information on a label on the disc drive for
future reference!

Data stored on discs cannot be regarded as
having an infinite life. Dust and other
particles build up over a period of time and
can conspire to render a disc unreadable.
Although there is frequent mention in this
guide about the need for backup copies, the

user should also periodically - say once every couple of years - consider making a duplicate copy of important discs, and of then using the original disc as a scratchpad disc for non-important material.

Discs vary in cost - at the time of writing they can be purchased for between £1 and £5. As with all things, you get what you pay for. The expensive discs have been stringently tested and usually come with a lifetime guarantee; they should be considered for serious software development. Cheaper discs certainly have their place, but should not normally be regarded as having undergone such stringent testing. Quantity purchasing - even as little as ten at a time - can bring useful savings as opposed to buying discs singly; forming a co-operative with other users, and buying fifty or a hundred discs together is probably the most cost-effective.

If you have occasion to send discs through the post, do use the special ´floppy mailers´ which have extra strength - or use a square of hardboard behind the disc. NEVER attach the disc to a letter or other material with paperclips.

FORMATTING NEW DISCS

(ref. *4)

Each new disc is like a ´music´ record
without its grooves. Before it can be used
the magnetic surface must be organised into
´tracks´ and ´sectors´.
This is done by the computer using a utility
program normally supplied with the disc
drive. The disc containing this program
should be kept in a safe place at all times
and you should keep a backup copy.

1. Insert UTILITY or FORMATTING disc in the
drive and type:

        *FORM40   (RETURN)

2. Remove the formatting disc when the drive
stops, before typing anything.

3. Insert the new disc in the drive.

4. You are asked
   ON WHICH DRIVE DO YOU WISH TO FORMAT

5. As a single drive is numerical DRIVE 0,
type in 0.
   When using dual drives you may format on
´0´ or ´1´

NOTE

At stage number 5 you may see the message
    Disc already formatted! Are you sure ?

This is to check that you do not
accidentally reformat a disc with precious
data on it, SO PLEASE CHECK! If you are
sure that you wish to erase everything on
this disc, then press ´Y´ and formatting
will continue as above. Pressing ´N´ will
abort the FORMAT operation. Remember -
better safe than sorry!

6. Following the Beeps and Burps the program
will ask you
        DO YOU WISH TO FORMAT ANOTHER DISC

7. If ´NO´, then type N (this ends the
procedure).

8. If ´YES´, type Y.

9. You will be returned to the original ´ON
WHICH DRIVE´ message.

10. CHANGE THE DISC BEFORE TYPING 0

USING DISCS

READING THE DIRECTORY

As stated before, the machine should be in DFS mode or can be returned to this mode by (BREAK) or *DISC.

The first step is to ensure that the disc is located in the drive correctly and that the gate or switch is closed.

It is useful to be aware of the disc´s contents as program names used in the LOAD command must be exact. The disc maintains its own catalogue of the names, and these program names can be read by using the command

*CAT (RETURN)

This will print the catalogue onto the screen.

To obtain a printed copy of the disc catalogue, type

VDU2 (RETURN)
*CAT (RETURN)
VDU3 (RETURN)

Some discs will have !BOOT in the catalogue. This enables the disc to be BOOTed into operation. (See Command words)

16

DELETING A PROGRAM FROM DISC

If you are certain that a program is **definitely** no longer required, then it is good housekeeping to remove it as soon as possible. As a general rule, **never** delete someone else's program unless you have their assurance that it is not needed!

1.   Insert the disc into the disc drive.

2.   Check the catalogue as shown before.

3.   Identify the program name.

4.   Type *DELETE program name - exactly as it appears on the catalogue.

5.   Press RETURN

The program will now be deleted from the disc.

DISC ECONOMY

As programs are stored on disc, varying
amounts of disc space are left unused within
the different sectors. It is sound practice
to regularly ´collect up´ or ´compact´ all
of these unused sectors and to make them
available for subsequent storage of new
programs, in order to attempt to avoid the
frustrating ´DISC FULL´ message which
inevitably appears when you have no spare,
formatted, disc to hand.

1.   Insert the disc into the disc drive.

2.   Type *COMPACT 0

3.   Press RETURN.

As compacting takes place, the files on the
disc are displayed on the screen, and all
unused space is then freed for subsequent
saving of programs.

PROTECTING PROGRAMS and FILES

Apart from the ´catch-all´ method of disc protection mentioned on page 12, it is possible to safeguard individual programs or files from being deliberately or inadvertently over-written or deleted. This is especially useful in situations where the disc must be allowed to have new or updated files written to it, but where the main program needs some security.

1. Insert disc into disc drive.

2. Type *ACCESS program name L
    (Ensure, as always, that the program name is written exactly as is recorded on the disc.)

3. Press RETURN.

This LOCKS the program, and it cannot be deleted or overwritten.

If, subsequently, you do require to modify· or remove the program, it can be ´unlocked´ by typing
            *ACCESS program name

Note that this locking will **not** prevent the program being destroyed by commands such as *FORM40.

LOADING FROM DISC (ref *4)

1. Type
        LOAD "program name"   (RETURN)
(This operation will display no screen
message, though you will hear the drive in
operation.)

2. The cursor   >   will return when the
program is loaded. You may now type RUN
(RETURN)   to   get   the   program   to   run.
Alternatively, you may type LIST (RETURN) to
see the individual program lines.

A more commonly-used method to load and run
a program is to CHAIN it.

1. Type
        CHAIN "program name"   (RETURN)
This command will LOAD and RUN the program
automatically and no messages will appear.

SAVING TO DISC   (ref. *4)

If you think that the machine is in TFS mode
DO NOT change to DFS using BREAK as you will
lose the program that is in the memory and
that you wish to save. In this situation
always use the *DISC command to change
filing systems.

If BREAK is, however, accidentally pressed,
then typing OLD (RETURN) will usually
restore the program.

1. Ensure that the disc is located in the
drive correctly and the gate is closed.

2. *CAT the disc to check that you are not
trying to save a program by a name that
already exists. This is extremely important
as the computer will happily overwrite
programs already stored without giving any
indication that this has been done!)

3. Type SAVE "program name" (RETURN)
   (maximum of seven characters in the name)

4. When the cursor > appears the program is
saved.

   What about a backup copy on another disc?

PROBLEMS

Error messages that may be displayed are:

Read/Write error at sector xx
Can´t Extend
Disc Full

(Check these in ERROR MESSAGE section)

Record and Return

The machine is still in TFS mode. Use ESCAPE and *DISC and repeat saving procedure.

If the drive makes a protracted whirring and the cursor refuses to return, this will usually be caused by
1. No disc in the disc drive!
2. The gate of the drive not being closed.

Press BREAK. This will halt the saving and allow you to check the disc and drive are set up correctly. To regain the program you are trying to save type OLD (RETURN).
This may not work and you will have to reload the program you wish to save and repeat the whole procedure.

```
*************************
*   FROM NOW ON IT IS   *
*    ASSUMED THAT THE   *
*  READER UNDERSTANDS   *
*  THAT EACH COMMAND    *
*      ENTRY MUST BE    *
* FOLLOWED BY (RETURN)  *
*************************
```

C O P Y I N G   P R O G R A M S

WARNING! The user should check if a program
is copyright before copying.

The rules of copyright make it a
questionable legal situation if a user wants
to copy, for the purposes of providing a
backup, a program that he has legally
purchased. The current ´protection devices´
which are used to prevent illegal copying
can often prevent backups being made.

However when copying is both legal and
possible the user should find the following
procedures useful.

Procedures for copying are dependent on the
type of program structure. The structures
that are normally encountered are:

1. Single part BASIC programs

2. Multiple part BASIC programs

3. Mixed BASIC and MACHINE CODE programs

4. MACHINE CODE programs

Some changes in the procedures are needed
when changing the storage medium between
LOADing and SAVEing.

CROSS COPY

TAPE to DISC   and   DISC to TAPE

All the procedures listed in the following sections apply with the inclusion of the commands *TAPE or *DISC as are necessary to swop between the two filing systems between LOADing and SAVEing.

PROBLEMS

With certain programs written for the TFS-based machine you may find that when stored on disc the program will not RUN.

This is because the original program needs almost all of the machine's memory. As the DFS 'steals' some memory that is normally available to the user, it is likely to corrupt the program when it is transferred to the machine.

If this problem is encountered the user should refer to a local 'expert' for advice on 'moving programs down' in memory. (This procedure is beyond the scope of this guide.)

LOADING FROM DISC

Programs can be readily identified on **tape** as they follow each other in sequence and a simple command LOAD"" can be used. The machine will then load each program in turn as they are played by the tape.

The **disc**-based system requires a specific name to load programs, that is, LOAD"program name"

To check on the programs stored on a disc, follow this procedure:

1. *CAT the disc to see the names of the programs stored.

2. The names of all the programs on the disc are displayed.

It may be possible to identify the program you want at this stage.

If so ignore the next section.

Some disc systems operate a !BOOT or MENU program which can make identification of a program´s name much more difficult.

!BOOT AND MENU PROGRAMS

For full information on !BOOT programs, see
section 8; here we are simply concerned with
being able to identify program names for
subsequent copying.

A !BOOT program is set up by the program
writer and stored on the disc. It operates
when SHIFT and BREAK are pressed together.

If !BOOT is noted on the program catalogue,
use the command
              *TYPE !BOOT
to see the contents of the !BOOT program.

The contents of !BOOT are normally similar
to the following examples:

           10 CHAIN "program name"
                    or
              10 CHAIN "menu"
   (when a MENU program is on the disc.)

In the case of the first example, where a
specific program is CHAINed, it is likely
that this will be the program name you
require. This program can be loaded by the
command LOAD "program name".

In the second example, where a MENU program
is loaded and run, the display will be of a
menu of programs which will be loaded and
run following a single key press. To obtain
the specific program name that you require,
carry out the following procedure.

Use the !BOOT function to get the MENU
program running.

From the screen display identify the program
that you require and note the key press
needed to run this program.

Break out of the MENU program by pressing
either BREAK or CONTROL/BREAK.
Reload the MENU program and type LIST.

There will be a section of the listing
something like this:

```
 90 INPUT X$
100 IF X$="1" CHAIN"PROG1"
110 IF X$="2" CHAIN"PROG2"
```

Match the key press you have noted with
the value of X$ (1 or 2 etc.) and you will
see the name of the program that you require
(PROG1 or PROG2).

You may now LOAD the program in the usual
manner, by entering
          LOAD "program name"

LOADING FROM TAPE OR DISC

Single and multiple parts can now be copied in the following manner.

Load the program by the specific name you have identified, and LIST it. (Use CONTROL N to page the listing)

If the following commands are not present, or if you are sure the program is single-part, then use the simple LOAD and SAVE procedure.

If the listing contains lines such as:

*RUN"name"   CHAIN"name"   *LOAD"name"

then the program is stored in several sections. (See ´Multiple part programs´)

Single part programs

LOAD the program and SAVE it under an appropriate name.

Remember that only seven characters may be used in DFS.

Multiple part programs

Load the first part of the program as above and LIST the program.

1. Make a note of the appropriate line which accesses the second part of the program - for example, CHAIN"name". Bear in mind the fact that this first program could call up several different programs, so check all lines to ensure that you have identified all of the CHAIN"name" lines and names.

2. This first part can now be saved to the storage system. (Remember that tape storage systems require the various program parts to be in the correct order!)

3. If the noted line was CHAIN"name" then you may now LOAD"name" as normal and proceed to SAVE it under the **same name** - that is, the name that is CHAINed from the first program part.

4. If the line contains either *LOAD"name" or *RUN"name" then you are dealing with a combined BASIC and MACHINE CODE program.

Note the name of the program that is *RUN or *LOADed and save the BASIC as for SINGLE PART programs.

Then refer to the MACHINE CODE COPYING section as *RUN and *LOAD are commands used to load machine code which is not stored or saved in the same way as BASIC.

MACHINE CODE COPYING

Any commands referred to in this section are
more fully explained in the section ´Systems
commands´.

These programs are run by

1. The command *RUN being typed in from the
keyboard.

2. The command *RUN being used by a !BOOT or
MENU program on a disc.

3. The command *LOAD being used to load the
program   and   then   using   the   command
CALL &(number) to start the program running.

As machine code is stored in a different
manner to BASIC, it is not possible to load
this type of program in the normal fashion.
The following procedure must be carried out,
having first identified the name of the
machine code program.

Loading machine code (*5)

1   Type *OPT 1,2

2   Type *LOAD"prog name"

3   Message appears

    (when loaded from tape)
prog name nb   yyyy xxxx ffff zzzz

    (when loaded from disc)
prog name xxxx   zzzz yyyy loc

Where:

nb   is the number of blocks of code

yyyy is the length in bytes

xxxx is the start address

ffff is the finish address

zzzz is the run address

loc   is the disc location of the program

Saving machine code

This form of program requires special commands to save:

  Type *SAVE"prog name" xxxx + yyyy   zzzz

Where:

xxxx   is the load address

yyyy   is the length of code in bytes

zzzz   is the run address

 N.B. (xxxx and zzzz are often the same numbers)

NOTE
    Remember to use the same name to save the program as was used to load it, when dealing with multi-part programs.

S Y S T E M   C O M M A N D S

*DISC
To enter Disc Filing System

*TAPE
To enter Tape Filing System

LOAD"program name"
To load a program without running it.
N.B. THE QUOTE MARKS (" ") ARE ESSENTIAL.

LOAD""
To load the next program in sequence from
tape.
N.B. Does **NOT** work on DFS.

RUN
To run a program already in the machine.

CHAIN"program name"
As with LOAD but also RUNs the specified
program.

LIST
If a program is resident in the machine it
is possible to LIST it.
Standard LIST will run up the screen at high
speed.
To page the listing use the next command.

LIST and **(CONTROL N)**
Type LIST and then hold down CONTROL and press N before using RETURN.
This will show the listing a page at a time. Use SHIFT to move to next page.

(CONTROL O) Disables page mode.

LIST 280
This will list the BASIC line number 280 only.

LIST 280,450
This will list all lines between 280 and 450.

LIST ,450
This will list all lines from the beginning to line 450.

LIST 450,
This lists all lines from 450 to the end.

LISTO
This command - which may be used in conjunction with any of the previous LIST commands - is followed by a single digit, and causes spaces to be inserted into the listing to make it more readable. The command takes effect from the next LIST instruction.
LISTO0 causes NO inserted spaces
LISTO1 causes a space after the line number
LISTO2 causes spaces during FOR..NEXT loops
LISTO4 causes spaces during REPEAT..UNTIL loops.

LISTO (continued)

It is possible to combine the effects of
this command by adding together the digits
to obtain the required effect - so to have
spaces after the line number AND during
FOR..NEXT loops you should use 1 and 2,
making a digit of 3; the command would
therefore be LISTO3.

*LOAD

You may have found a line of listing which
includes the command *LOAD"prog name".
This command tells the machine to load a
block of machine code.
This indicates that the BASIC program has
sections of machine code which are used by
the command CALL xxxx (where xxx is an
address in memory)

*SAVE

The blocks of machine code mentioned in
*LOAD are saved by this command in the
following format:

*SAVE "prog name" xxxx + yyyy zzzz

Where:
xxxx   is the load address

yyyy   is the length of code in bytes

zzzz   is the run address

(xxxx and zzzz are often the same numbers)

All this data is obtained using *OPT1,2.

*RUN
Certain programs will only be written in
code. Therefore they are usually loaded and
run by this command.

*OPT 1,2
This command has no obvious effect on the
machine.
It should be used to obtain the LOAD
ADDRESS, LENGTH IN BYTES and RUN ADDRESS of
machine code programs. For example,
    *OPT 1,2
    *LOAD" prog name"

The following message will appear:

  prog name nb yyyy xxxx ffff zzzz

Where:

nb   is the number of blocks of code

yyyy   is the length in bytes

xxxx   is the start address

ffff   is the finish address

zzzz   is the run address

N.B.
All these numbers are in **hexadecimal** form.
Where 8 numbers are shown, only the last 4
are significant.

BOOTING   !BOOT

If you have saved programs to disc you may
wish to run them with a minimum of command
entries.

This is especially useful when the programs
are likely to be used by people with little
confidence at handling the computer, or
alternatively when there are a variety of
programs which could be used, but where
knowing the individual names of each program
would be unwieldy. This facility is
available on disc only.

A program can be loaded and run by a !BOOT
routine, which then merely requires the
CONTROL and BREAK keys to be pressed.

This program is, in fact, often a MENU
program which displays the contents of the
disc and allows selection of one of a
variety of different programs.

*BUILD !BOOT

This command is used to build a !BOOT routine.

1. Type *BUILD !BOOT

The number 1 appears

2. Type CHAIN"whatever program you wish to auto run"

3. Press RETURN

4. Press ESCAPE

5. Type *OPT 4,3

The routine !BOOT is now stored on disc; item 5 sets the EXEC option, which is essential for !BOOT to work.

Use !BOOT by holding down SHIFT and tapping the BREAK key.

P R I N T E R   C O M M A N D S

(*8)

VDU 2
This is a BASIC instruction which is normally within a program.
This command directs all printed output to the printer.

VDU 3
This is also BASIC and cancels the VDU 2 command.

CONTROL B
This command to divert output to the printer is entered in direct mode as follows:
        Hold down CONTROL and press B
The command has the same effect as VDU 2

CONTROL C
This command, to revert to screen output, is entered in direct mode by holding down CONTROL and pressing C.
This has the same effect as VDU 3.

This is possibly most frequently used to obtain a hard copy of the disc directory:

1. Hold CONTROL and press B
2. Type *CAT
3. Hold CONTROL and press C

W A Y S   O U T

Occasionally, the computer will manage to get itself into the situation whereby it is unable to accept any response from the keyboard. This could be due to a variety of reasons - almost always, however, to poor programming by the program writer.

There are four stages of rectifying this situation - the fourth, and most drastic being to switch the computer off! - but commercial software writers will usually have ´programmed out´ the first two options, in order to prevent accidental stopping of the program whilst in use. The usual effect of hitting these keys in these cases is to restart the program.

1. **ESCAPE**
Pressing this key should stop all operations unless the machine is instructed to ignore ESCAPE.

2. **BREAK**
As with ESCAPE, but exercise caution! This will cause the program in memory to be lost unless OLD is **immediately** typed in.

41

If these keys will not halt the operation
then use

3. **CONTROL BREAK** (hold down CONTROL and
press BREAK)

The **BBC Micro 32k** message will appear.

This should reset the machine and will
require the OLD command to restore the
program. Any programmed function keys will
lose their values.

4. In extreme cases - fortunately, these are
very rare - switching the computer off,
waiting a few seconds, and then switching
the computer back on is the only
alternative.

OLD
Following an accidental BREAK the program
may stop operation.

RUN will not work unless the machine can be
re-organised to the start of the program.

The command OLD should achieve this.

However, following OLD a message:

Bad Program

may be seen. This will mean reloading the
program before RUN will work.

D F S   C O M M A N D S

THE FOLLOWING HAVE BEEN DEALT WITH ABOVE:

  *SAVE   *BUILD

  *LOAD   !BOOT

****

*ACCESS "prog name"(L)
This locks the file "prog name" and prevents
overwriting.

*ACCESS "prog name"
This unlocks "prog name".

*BACKUP X Y
This command must be preceded by *ENABLE and
will back up the whole disc where X is the
source disc and Y is the destination disc.
If you have only one disc drive, this can be
0 to 0; you will be informed by the machine
when to take out and replace the disc in the
disc drive.
See also *ENABLE

*CAT
This command is used to find the names of all programs stored on a disc or a tape.
Sadly it is of little use on a tape system as it requires the whole tape to play through before displaying the catalogue.
With a disc system it will display all programs on the disc unless some ingenious locking device has been placed on a piece of commercial software.

*COMPACT X
This will squeeze up all the programs on drive X leaving all free space at the end. This is well worth trying if you get a ´Disc full´ message.

*COPY X Y "prog name"
This copies prog name from drive X to drive Y. (can be 0 to 0)

*DELETE "prog name"
This will delete prog name from the disc.

*DESTROY *.prog*
As above but this will delete all program beginning ´prog´.
See also *ENABLE

*DRIVE
This is used to change the default drive if twin drives are used. Type *DRIVE1 to switch over to drive 1, and *DRIVE0 to revert to drive 0.

*ENABLE
This must be used immediately before entering the *BACKUP or *DESTROY commands; its effect lasts only for one operation, and thus it must be re-keyed if subsequent similar operations are required.

*FORM40
This command loads the formatting program from the utility disc.

*HELP
This is used to get information on the ROMs fitted to the machine.

*TITLE fred
This is used to name the disc ´fred´.

*TYPE
This can be used to read the program !BOOT which is not readable by LIST.

E R R O R   M E S S A G E S

(*10)

Program related

Several of the following error messages
could be caused by a shortage of memory
space when running a program designed for a
tape system. The disc interface uses some of
the memory for work space. These errors are
marked *

Bad MODE
This shows that a change mode call is not
allowed or that there is not enough memory
to operate that mode.   *

Bad DIM
There is a mistake in a DIM statement. *

Bad Program
This indicates that the machine is unable to
locate the beginning of the program
following a break. It is also given if you
attempt to LOAD a block of machine code as
BASIC.

Block
This comes when the TFS fails to read a
section of tape. It is possible to rewind
the tape and overwrite the block or try a
backup copy of the tape.

Data
As with BLOCK there is a tape fault.

DIM space
As with Bad DIM *

Escape
The escape key has been pressed to interrupt
the program.

Error at line
There is some error in the program at   line
xxx. LIST xxx and try to work it out.

Missing "
You   have   typed   in   the command without   a
quote around the file name.

Mistake
The   machine   doesn´t   understand   the   junk
you´ve   just   typed   in!   This   could   be a
simple as typing in an instruction in lower
case - list, instead of LIST, for example.

No room
There   is not enough memory to carry out the
program   *

No such line
The program has referred to a line number
that does not exist. Usually from GOSUB or
GOTO.

No such variable
The program has referred to a variable that
has not been defined. One common cause is
incorrectly entering a variable in, for
example, lower case after is has been
originally defined in upper case.
Alternatively, variables with ´meaningful´
names - such as TOTAL or SURNAME$ - could
simply have been mistyped on one occasion.
Confusion between zero and the letter O, or
one and the letter I is also a common cause.

Syntax error
The line has been typed in incorrectly. A
frequent cause in complex lines is the
omission of a single bracket.

DISC ERRORS

NOT ENABLED
You have attempted a function that requires
*ENABLE before the command.

CATALOGUE FULL
You have attempted to save more than 31
files on a disc.

DRIVE FAULT XX AT YY/ZZ
The drive has found a blank spot on the disc
at sector YY track ZZ. This indicates that
the disc medium is corrupted.

DISK FULL
There is no more room on this disc. Try the
*COMPACT command.

WRITE PROTECTED or DISC READ ONLY
The disc has a write protect tab and cannot
be written to. This occurs if you try to
save on a disc of commercial programs.

INVALID FILENAME

Normally that you have tried to save a program with a filename of more than 7 letters.

FILE NOT FOUND

You have tried to load a program that has a different name, is on another disc - or you can´t type! Check your typing first!

FILE LOCKED

The program name you have tried to save already exists and is locked. See *ACCESS.

CAN´T EXTEND

Occurs when a random access file has no space left to include additional data. If this occurs after modifying a program and attempting to resave it with the same name then either *DELETE the original version or, safer, save the new version under a different name.

M I N I M U M
A B B R E V I A T I O N S

(*11)

Where no abbreviation is given please use command in full.

LOAD""	LO.""	*BUILD	*BU.
CHAIN""	CH.""	*COMPACT	*COM.
LIST	L.	*COPY	*COP.
OLD	O.	*HELP	*H.
*CAT	*.	*LOAD	*L.
*ACCESS	*A.	*SAVE	*S.
*ENABLE	*EN.	*OPT	*O.
*BACKUP	*BAC.	*RUN	*R.

ALTHOUGH IT IS OBVIOUSLY QUICKER TO USE THESE SHORT FORMS IT CAN LEAD TO ERRORS IF YOU ARE NOT USED TO THIS FORM OF COMMAND ENTRY.

51

C O M M O N   P R O B L E M S

Most operational problems the user may
encounter have been dealt with in the
relevant section of the guide.

Screen stalling

Many software writers include routines in
their software which will print out results
or worksheets etc. When one of these
routines is being run the printer must be
switched ON LINE as the micro is attempting
to send data.

In the event of the printer being OFF LINE
or not even connected the screen display of
the program will stall.

The same problem may occur if you have
accidentally pressed CONTROL B prior to
LISTing a program.

It is possible to switch the printer on and
the micro will then be able to continue to
send data to the printer.
If you have no printer connected it will be
possible to ESCAPE, press CONTROL C and
restart LISTing.

Loss of programs from storage (backups)

The loss of a program or data from a storage medium can be a problem. It is very important that users get into the habit of recording each program twice. This BACKUP copy may save a lot of bad language if someone deletes your favourite example of your programming ability.

If you also use the micro for data storage with a database it is worth saving data at frequent intervals as people are fond of removing the plug from the wall just as you near the end of a mammoth data entry session.

Incorrect use of disc drive

If you do not put a disc in the drive before using a drive command (SAVE"prog" etc.) then you will find that the micro attempts to load data by spinning the drive. To get out of this situation you must use the BREAK command and if needed the OLD command to restore your program.

Disc medium corruption

If you get repeated problems with a disc recover as many programs as possible and store them elsewhere. Then try to re-format the disc using *FORM40.

R E F E R E N C E S (*n)

The following references will link this guide to the official BBC User Guide. However, as the User Guide has seen many variations it is not possible to be accurate with page or section numbers.

REF. NO.	BBC User Guide
*1	Section 1
*2	Section 35 p. 393
*3	Section 35 p. 391
*4	All these refs. are generally dealt with in the User´s Guide issued with a disc drive.
*5	Section 35 p. 393
*6	Section 35 p. 392

REF. NO.	BBC User Guide
*7	Section 33 All the KEYWORDS or COMMANDS recognised by the BBC are listed with explanations.
*8	Appendix p. 507
*9	These commands are not listed in any single place in the Guide.
*10	Section 46 p. 474
*11	Section 47 p. 483

I N D E X